Coasts

by Sheila Anderson

first step non-fiction

Lerner Books · London · New York · Minneapolis

What is a **coast?**

It is a kind of **landform.**

A coast is where water
meets land.

The edge of the **sea** is the coast.

Some coasts are rocky.

Waves crash against the rocks.

Some coasts have sandy **beaches.**

Waves roll onto the beach.

Island coasts may have
black sand.

Others have white sand.

Animals look for food on the coast.

Plants grow by the water's edge.

People live on coasts.

People look for shells in the sand.

There are many things to
do on the coast.

Would you like to explore
the coast?

Ripples

Have you seen ripples like these in the sand on the beach? You can feel them with your fingers or toes. Waves make ripples under the water and on the shore. As waves move towards the shore, they pick up sand from the bottom of the sea and carry it along. The waves leave the sand at the shore. The sand forms lines. Each wave brings a little more sand and adds another line, creating ripples.

Coast Facts

 Sandy coasts are called beaches. The sand on beaches is made of rocks and shells that have been broken up into tiny pieces.

 Waves carry sand from the ocean floor up onto beaches.

 The sand on beaches can be white, brown, black and even pink.

 Black sand is made from broken down volcanic rocks.

Sand can be used to make glass.

 Some of the animals that live on or near coasts are crabs, snails, mussels, starfish, seals, dolphins, sea lions, turtles, birds, worms and sharks.

 Rock pools are small pockets of water on rocky coasts. Sea plants and animals live in rock pools.

Glossary

 beaches – sandy or pebbly shores of seas or lakes

 coast – the land next to a sea or ocean

 island – a piece of land that has water on all sides

 landform – a natural feature of the Earth's surface

 sea – a large area of salt water that covers nearly three quarters of the Earth

Index

All rights reserved. International copyright secured. No part of this book may be reproduced, stored in a retrieval system or transmitted in any form or by any means – electronic, mechanical, photocopying, recording or otherwise – without the prior written permission of Lerner Publishing Group, Inc., except for the inclusion of brief quotations in an acknowledged review.

The photographs in this book are used with the permission of: © Photodisc Royalty-free/Getty Images, pp 2, 4, 5, 18, 22 (second from top, bottom); © Darrell Guin/Stone/Getty Images, pp 3, 22 (second from bottom); © John Kreul/Independent Picture Service, p 6; © Marli Miller/Visuals Unlimited, p 7; © Theo Allofs/Stone/Getty Images, pp 8, 22 (top); © istockphoto.com/ATVG, p 9; © Steve Vidler/SuperStock, pp 10, 22 (middle); © Darren Robb/Stone/Getty Images, p 11; © age fotostock/SuperStock, pp 12, 13; © Richard Nowitz/National Geographic/Getty Images, p 14; © Mirek Weichsel/First Light/Getty Images, p 15; © Paul Avis/Taxi/Getty Images, p 16; © Eyewire Royalty-free/Getty Images, p 17.

Front Cover: © Rich Reid/NationalGeographic/Getty Images.

First published in the United Kingdom in 2010 by
Lerner Books,
Dalton House,
60 Windsor Avenue,
London SW19 2RR

Website address: www.lernerbooks.co.uk

This edition was updated and edited for UK publication by Discovery Books Ltd., First Floor, 2 College Street, Ludlow, Shropshire SY8 1AN

British Library Cataloguing in Publication Data
Anderson, Sheila
Coasts. - 2nd ed. - (First step nonfiction. Landforms)
1. Coasts - Juvenile literature 2. Coastal ecology -
Juvenile literature
I. Title
551.4'57

ISBN-13: 978 0 7613 4365 3

Printed in China

First published in the United States of America in 2008
Text copyright © 2008 by Lerner Publishing Group, Inc.